BIOGEOLOGY

By Christina Earley

A Stingray Book

SEAHORSE
PUBLISHING

Teaching Tips for Caregivers and Teachers:

This Hi-Lo book features high-interest subject matter that will appeal to all readers in intermediate and middle school grades. It may be enjoyed by students reading at or above grade level as well as by those who are looking for age-appropriate themes matched with a less challenging reading level. Hi-Lo books are ideal for ELL readers, too.

Each book appeals to a striving reader's age and maturity level. Opportunities are provided for students to read words they already know while encountering a limited number of new, high-interest vocabulary words. With these supports in place, students will read more fluently while increasing reading comprehension. Use the following suggestions to help students grow as readers.

- Encourage the student to read independently at home.
- Encourage the student to practice reading aloud.
- Encourage activities that require reading.
- Establish a regular reading time.
- Have the student write questions about what they read.

Teaching Tips for Teachers:

Before Reading

- Ask, "What do I know about this topic?"
- Ask, "What do I want to learn about this topic?"

During Reading

- Ask, "What is the author trying to teach me?"
- Ask, "How is this like something I already know?"

After Reading

- Discuss how the text features (headings, index, etc.) help with understanding the topic.
- Ask, "What interesting or fun fact did you learn?"

TABLE OF CONTENTS

BIOGEOLOGY. 4

PLANTS SPEED EROSION 6

PLANTS SLOW EROSION 8

ANIMALS SPEED EROSION. 10

ANIMALS SLOW EROSION 12

HUMANS SPEED EROSION. 14

HUMANS SLOW EROSION 16

CAREER: GEOBIOLOGIST 18

INVESTIGATE: PLANTS AND EROSION 20

THE SCIENTIFIC METHOD 21

SCIENTIST SPOTLIGHT .21

GLOSSARY 22

INDEX 23

AFTER READING QUESTIONS. 23

ABOUT THE AUTHOR 24

BIOGEOLOGY

Biogeology is the study of how Earth's living things **interact** with Earth's nonliving things.

Plants and animals are living things. They need nonliving things, such as water and minerals, to live and grow.

As life-forms use natural resources, they change Earth.

As Earth changes, living organisms **adapt**.

FUN FACTS

Biology is the study of life. Geology is the study of Earth. Biogeology focuses on how the two affect each other.

Elephants get salt and minerals from the soil.

PLANTS SPEED EROSION

Plants change the land through **weathering** and **erosion**.

Moss that grows on rock takes minerals from the rock.

The moss's roots grow into small cracks in the rock. The cracks get bigger, and the rock breaks apart.

After a very long time, the rock's surface becomes soil. Water and wind may carry the soil away to a new place.

Growing plants can crack and break rock.

PLANTS SLOW EROSION

Plants can also slow down weathering and erosion.

As a tree grows, it traps pieces of rock and soil.

The tree's roots catch **sediment** being carried by water.

Over time, sediment collects around the roots and becomes packed. It is harder to erode.

FUN FACTS

A plant's leaves catch sand being blown by wind, making small hills.

ANIMALS SPEED EROSION

Animals change Earth's surface, too.

Weathering happens when snails scrape rocks to eat algae.

Burrowing animals contribute to erosion. They make mounds and holes. Their digging loosens the soil, making it easier for wind and water to carry it away.

ANIMALS SLOW EROSION

Animals can also slow down weathering and erosion.

Some animals change the land by **depositing** material.

Beavers build dams that block the flow of a stream or river. This creates a pond. The slowed river deposits sediment at the bottom of the pond.

World's Largest Beaver Dam

The dam is one-half mile (850 meters) long.

FUN FACTS

The world's largest beaver dam is in Canada. It can be seen from space!

HUMANS SPEED EROSION

Human activity causes erosion to happen faster than it does through natural processes.

People cut down trees to make space for buildings and farms. Clearing land scrapes away plants that protected the soil.

Machines dig into Earth's surface to make roads and bury pipes. This exposes soil to erosion from water or wind.

FUN FACTS

The first evidence of humans moving Earth's soil is from 40,000 years ago.

HUMANS SLOW EROSION

Humans can also prevent weathering and erosion.

Farmers fight soil erosion by choosing not to **plow** in steep, wet areas.

Instead, some farmers make **terraces**. They look like wide steps on the sides of hills.

Terraces trap rainwater. It stays for a long time so plants can use it to grow.

CAREER: GEOBIOLOGIST

Geobiologists study how physical changes to Earth affect plants and animals.

They might research how oxygen levels in the **atmosphere** affect the growth of ocean plants or other organisms.

Some geobiologists are studying tiny organisms in the Arctic that could provide clues about where to find life on other planets.

INVESTIGATE: PLANTS AND EROSION

Materials:

- 2 aluminum loaf pans (about 8 in. x 3 in. x 3 in./ 20 cm x 8 cm x 8 cm)
- Potting soil
- Radish seeds or other small, quick-growing seeds
- Sharp tool such as scissors or a knife
- Aluminum cake pan large enough to fit both loaf pans inside
- Short plastic container to use as a prop
- Full-size watering can with rain spout

Procedure:

(1) Fill loaf pans with soil. Leave a little space at the top. Plant seeds very close together in one pan. The other pan will have no seeds.

(2) Have an adult use the sharp tool to make drainage holes along the bottom edge of each long side of both loaf pans.

(3) Put the loaf pans inside the cake pan and set in a sunny spot. Water both loaf pans once per day.

(4) When plants are about four inches (ten centimeters) tall, test for soil erosion. Have an adult use the scissors or knife to make two vertical cuts halfway down a short side of each loaf pan. Fold down to expose the soil.

(5) Empty and clean the cake pan. Use the plastic container to prop up the uncut short side of the loaf pan without the plants. The cut side should lean into the cake pan. Use the watering can to simulate rain over the soil. Observe.

(6) Repeat the test with the loaf pan that has plants. Observe. Did the plants hold more soil and prevent or decrease erosion?

THE SCIENTIFIC METHOD

- Ask a question.
- Gather information and observe.
- Make a hypothesis or guess the answer.
- Experiment and test your hypothesis, or guess.
- Analyze your test results.
- Modify your hypothesis, if necessary.
- Make a conclusion.

SCIENTIST SPOTLIGHT

Nora Noffke is an American geobiologist. She found evidence that bacterial life existed on Earth billions of years ago. By looking at photos taken by the NASA rover *Curiosity*, she also found potential signs of ancient life on Mars. This shows that Mars must have been warmer and wetter about four million years ago. Noffke is currently a professor at Old Dominion University in Virginia.

GLOSSARY

adapt (uh-DAPT): to survive by changing and adjusting to the environment

atmosphere (AT-muhs-feer): the mixture of gases that surrounds a planet; all the air between the surface of a planet and outer space

burrowing (BUR-oh-ing): digging to make a tunnel or hole in the ground, especially as a home for a rabbit or other small animal

depositing (di-PAH-zi-ting): placing or laying down, especially to transport something to a new place

erosion (i-ROH-zhuhn): the process by which rocks, soil, and other materials are worn down and carried away by wind, water, or ice

interact (in-tur-AKT): to react to one another; to become involved with or affect others

plow (plou): to break up soil and prepare it for planting

sediment (SED-uh-muhnt): bits of rock, sand, soil, and other materials that get picked up by water, wind, or ice before they are deposited in a new place

terraces (TER-is-es): flat areas made on a hillside or other slope

weathering (WETH-ur-ing): the breaking down or dissolving of rocks and minerals

INDEX

beaver(s) 12, 13

erosion 6, 8, 10, 12, 14, 16, 20

farms/farmers 14, 16

humans 14, 15, 16

minerals 4, 5, 6

moss 6

sediment 8, 12

water 4, 6, 8, 10, 14, 20

weathering 6, 8, 10, 12, 16

wind 6, 9, 10, 14

AFTER READING QUESTIONS

1. What is biogeology?

2. How do animals make changes to the land?

3. Why is it important to learn how plants, animals, and humans change Earth?

ABOUT THE AUTHOR

Christina Earley lives in South Florida with her husband, son, and dog. Her favorite subject in school was science. She enjoys learning the science behind the world around her, such as how roller coasters work. She loves mint chocolate chip ice cream and mermaids.

Written by: Christina Earley
Design by: Kathy Walsh
Editor: Kim Thompson

Library of Congress PCN Data
Biogeology / Christina Earley
Earth and Space Science
ISBN 979-8-8873-5362-3 (hard cover)
ISBN 979-8-8873-5447-7 (paperback)
ISBN 979-8-8873-5532-0 (EPUB)
ISBN 979-8-8873-5617-4 (eBook)
Library of Congress Control Number: 2023930209

Printed in the United States of America.

Photographs/Shutterstock: Cover & Title pg: sondem, ju_see, Aksenova Nadezhd, amudsenh; p 4-23: amudsenh; p 4, 9, 11, 13, 15: Hlidskjalf; p 4:Ondrej Prosicky; p 5: Phubadee Na Songkhla; p 6: Nemeziya; p 7: Mila.LifeReporters; p 8: 010110010101101; p 9: Elisa Manzati; p 10: Matt T Jackson, EcoPrint; p 11: panotthorn phuhual; p 12: O Brasil que poucos conhecem; p 13: Google World maps; p 14: Rich Carey; p 15: Vadim Ratnikov; p 16: kid315; p 18: EvgenyPlotnikov; p 19: AYA images; p 21: NASA@Wiki, Pixel-Shot

Seahorse Publishing Company

www.seahorsepub.com

Published in the United States
Seahorse Publishing
PO Box 771325
Coral Springs, FL 33077

SEAHORSE PUBLISHING